FLOWER FARMING FOR PROFIT

The Essential Handbook for Cut Flower Business

By Stella Robert

COPYRIGHT ©️2024 by [Stella Robert]

All rights reserved. No part of this publication may be reproduced, distributed, or transmitted in any form or by any means, including photocopying, recording, or other electronic or mechanical methods, without the prior written permission of the publisher, except in the case of brief quotations embodied in critical reviews and certain other noncommercial uses permitted by copyright law.

From the Heart of Stella Robert to the Readers.

Like Flowers in a field, our dreams may start small, but with dedication and perseverance, they can bloom into fields of endless possibilities.

In the garden of life, there are no shortcuts to success, but with patience, persistence, and a touch of creativity, even the smallest seed can grow into a towering sunflower, reaching for the sky.

As farmers of flowers, we are stewards of beauty. Let us tend to our gardens with love and reverence, knowing that in nurturing nature, we nourish our souls.

Table of Contents

INTRODUCTION

Flower farming is a profitable business not so many people know about, and when people even hear of flower farming, they wonder, "How do I make money from that?" Well, no one is to be blamed, as I (Stella Robert) was once like that. It wasn't until I stumbled upon the idea after searching for a job to no avail, even after completing my master's degree. All I heard from prospective employers was, "The space has been occupied, come back later."

Amidst this frustration, I discovered the captivating world of flower farming. Initially intrigued by its beauty, I soon realized its immense potential for generating income. What began as a leap of faith transformed into a thriving business venture, propelling me on a journey of entrepreneurship fueled by the allure of nature's finest creations.

In this book, I aim to share my journey and insights, offering a roadmap for those intrigued by the idea of flower farming but unsure of its profitability. Through practical advice, strategies, and firsthand experiences, I hope to demystify the notion that flower farming is merely a hobby, revealing its true potential as a lucrative and fulfilling enterprise.

Join me as we explore the untapped opportunities of flower farming, where passion and profit intersect in a harmonious symphony of nature and entrepreneurship. It's time to dispel the misconceptions and embrace the blossoming possibilities that await those daring enough to embark on this floral odyssey.

The Rise of Flower Farming as a Lucrative Business

In recent years, flower farming has emerged from the confines of quaint hobbyist gardens to claim its rightful place as a lucrative and dynamic business venture. Once relegated to the realms of romantic notions and backyard pastimes, flower farming has undergone a profound transformation, propelled by shifting consumer preferences, technological advancements, and a growing awareness of the economic opportunities inherent in cultivating blooms.

One of the driving forces behind the rise of flower farming as a profitable enterprise is the increasing demand for locally grown, sustainably sourced floral products. In an era marked by a heightened emphasis on environmental consciousness and ethical consumption, consumers are increasingly drawn to flowers cultivated with care and consideration for the planet. This shift has created a fertile market for small-scale flower farmers, offering them a platform to showcase their blooms and connect with eco-conscious consumers eager to support local growers.

Moreover, the advent of e-commerce and direct-to-consumer platforms has revolutionized the floral industry, by-passing traditional distribution channels and enabling flower farmers to reach a broader audience with ease. This democratization of the market has leveled the playing field, allowing small-scale growers to compete with larger producers on a more equitable footing. By leveraging digital platforms and social media channels, flower farmers can cultivate a loyal customer base and establish their brand presence without the need for costly marketing campaigns or intermediaries.

Additionally, the resurgence of interest in artisanal and specialty flowers has provided flower farmers with an opportunity to differentiate their products and command premium prices. From heirloom varieties to rare blooms, consumers are increasingly seeking out unique and distinctive floral offerings, creating niche markets ripe for exploration by enterprising growers. This diversification of product offerings not only enhances the aesthetic appeal of flower farms but also increases their revenue potential, as customers are willing to pay a premium for flowers that evoke a sense of rarity and exclusivity.

Furthermore, the rise of agritourism and farm-to-table experiences has presented flower farmers with an opportunity to diversify their revenue streams and engage with consumers in a more meaningful way. By offering on-farm workshops, floral design classes, and u-pick experiences, flower farmers can create immersive and memorable experiences that resonate with customers and foster a sense of connection to the land. These experiential offerings not only generate additional income but also strengthen the bond between farmer and consumer, fostering loyalty and advocacy within the community.

Understanding the Potential of the Flower Market

The flower market, a realm often associated with beauty and sentimentality harbors a wealth of economic potential awaiting exploration. Its roots stretch deep into history, evolving from the traditional cultural practices into a dynamic industry shaped by contemporary trends and consumer preferences.

Today, the demand for flowers extends far beyond mere decoration, encompassing a diverse array of occasions and lifestyles. From weddings and celebrations to everyday indulgence, flowers play a central role in enhancing our lives and environments. Moreover, the global nature of the flower trade presents opportunities for both local growers and international exporters to tap into an ever-expanding market.

However, navigating this landscape requires a nuanced understanding of seasonal variability, supply chain complexities, and competitive dynamics. Yet, with innovation and adaptation, entrepreneurs can unlock new avenues for growth, from value-added products for sustainable sourcing practices. Looking ahead, the future of the flower market shines bright with promise, offering fertile ground for those willing to embrace change and cultivate success in this blooming industry

Benefits and Challenges of flower farming

Flower farming for profit offers numerous benefits, including the opportunity for creative expression and connection with nature, as growers immerse themselves in the vibrant colors and fragrances of their blooms. Moreover, flower farming can be a financially rewarding endeavor, with high-value flowers commanding premium prices in local and global markets, providing growers with a steady source of income. Additionally, cultivating flowers can contribute to environmental sustainability by promoting biodiversity, supporting pollinator populations, and enhancing the ecological resilience of agricultural landscapes.

However, flower farming also presents several challenges.

- Seasonal variability and weather fluctuations can significantly impact crop yields, requiring growers to implement resilient cultivation practices and diversify their offerings to mitigate risks.
- Perishable nature of flowers necessitates careful post-harvest handling and storage techniques to maintain quality and extend shelf life, which can be labor-intensive and resource-intensive.
- Market dynamics, including competition from imports, fluctuating demand, and evolving consumer preferences, add complexity, requiring growers to stay agile, innovative, and adaptable to remain competitive in the industry.

Despite these challenges, the allure of flower farming endures, offering a harmonious blend of artistry, entrepreneurship, and stewardship that continues to attract growers seeking to cultivate beauty while simultaneously reaping financial rewards and contributing to the sustainable development of agricultural systems.

CHAPTER 1

Planning For Your Flower Farm

Starting a flower farm is an exciting venture that can be both rewarding and profitable. However, like any business endeavor, it requires careful planning to ensure success.

Importance of Planning

Planning helps you define your long-term vision and short-term objectives for your flower farm. It allows you to articulate what you want to achieve and how you will measure success.

Through planning, you can identify the resources required to start and operate your flower farm, including land, equipment, seeds, labor, and capital. This helps you allocate resources efficiently and avoid unnecessary expenses.

Planning allows you to anticipate potential challenges and risks that may arise in the course of establishing and running your flower farm. By identifying these risks early on, you can develop strategies to mitigate them and increase the likelihood of success.

A well-thought-out plan helps streamline operations and maximize efficiency in all aspects of your flower farm, from planting and harvesting to marketing and sales. This can lead to cost savings and higher profits in the long run.

Banks, investors, or other funding sources typically require a comprehensive business plan before providing financing for your flower farm. A solid plan demonstrates your commitment to the venture and your ability to manage it effectively, increasing your chances of securing funding.

Steps in Planning Your Flower Farm

- **Define Your Vision and Goals:** Start by defining your vision for the flower farm. What type of flowers do you want to grow? Are you targeting the local market, or do you have aspirations for broader distribution? Set specific, measurable goals that align with your vision.

- **Conduct Market Research:** Research the demand for flowers in your target market, including consumer preferences, trends, and pricing. Identify your target customers and competitors to understand the competitive landscape and opportunities for differentiation.

- **Choose a Suitable Location:** Select a location for your flower farm that provides the right climate, soil conditions, and access to water and sunlight for your chosen flower varieties. Consider factors such as proximity to markets, transportation infrastructure, and zoning regulations.

- **Develop a Crop Plan:** Based on your market research and chosen location, develop a crop plan outlining the types of flowers you will grow, their planting and harvesting schedules, and estimated yields. Consider factors such as seasonality, market demand, and production costs.

- **Create a Budget:** Prepare a detailed budget outlining the costs associated with starting and operating your flower farm, including land acquisition or lease, equipment purchases or rentals, seeds or bulbs, labor, utilities, marketing, and administrative expenses. Be sure to include both one-time startup costs and ongoing operational expenses.

- **Obtain Necessary Permits and Licenses:** Research and obtain any permits or licenses required to operate a flower farm in your area, such as agricultural permits, zoning approvals, water rights, and pesticide applicator certifications. Compliance with regulatory requirements is essential to avoid potential fines or penalties.

- **Develop a Marketing Plan:** Outline your marketing strategy for promoting and selling your flowers to customers. Consider various marketing channels, such as farmer's markets, florists, supermarkets, online platforms, and direct sales to consumers. Develop a branding strategy to differentiate your flower farm and attract customers.

- **Establish Production and Quality Standards:** Establish production practices and quality standards to ensure the consistent quality and freshness of your flowers. Implement proper crop rotation, irrigation, fertilization, pest and disease management, and post-harvest handling procedures to optimize yield and quality.

- **Build Relationships with Suppliers and Partners:** Identify suppliers for seeds, bulbs, fertilizers, pesticides, and other inputs needed for your flower farm. Establish relationships with reliable suppliers to ensure a steady and high-quality supply chain. Consider forming partnerships with florists, event planners, wedding venues, and other businesses to expand your market reach.

- **Develop a Risk Management Plan:** Identify potential risks to your flower farm, such as adverse weather conditions, pest infestations, crop failures, market fluctuations, and operational disruptions. Develop contingency plans and risk mitigation strategies to minimize the impact of these risks on your business operations.

- **Monitor and Evaluate Performance:** Regularly monitor and evaluate the performance of your flower farm against your goals and objectives. Track key performance indicators such as sales volume, revenue, production costs, profit margins, customer satisfaction, and market share. Use this data to make informed decisions and adjust your strategies as needed to improve business performance.

In conclusion, planning is essential for the success of your flower farm. By carefully considering each of the steps outlined above and developing a comprehensive plan, you can increase the likelihood of achieving your goals and building a thriving and sustainable flower farming business.

Assessing Resources and Skills For Flower Farming

Before embarking on the journey of flower farming, it's essential to assess the resources and skills you possess. This thorough evaluation ensures that you are well-equipped to establish and manage a successful flower farm. To assess your resources, these things are to be considered with their respective skills.

1. Land and Location

Assessment: Evaluate the availability and suitability of land for flower cultivation. Consider factors such as soil quality, drainage, sunlight exposure, and proximity to water sources.

Skills Needed: Basic knowledge of agricultural land assessment and understanding of soil types and their suitability for different flower varieties.

2. Financial Resources

Assessment: Determine your financial capacity to start and sustain a flower farm. Calculate startup costs, including land acquisition or lease, equipment, seeds, labor, and ongoing operational expenses.

Skills Needed: Financial planning and budgeting skills to accurately estimate costs, forecast revenue, and manage finances effectively. Ability to secure funding through savings, loans, grants, or investor partnerships.

3. Equipment and Infrastructure

Assessment: Assess the availability and condition of essential farming equipment and infrastructure, such as tractors, irrigation systems, greenhouse facilities, and storage buildings.

Skills Needed: Basic understanding of farm equipment operation and maintenance. Ability to identify equipment needs and prioritize investments based on farm size and production requirements.

4. Agricultural Knowledge

Assessment: Evaluate your knowledge of flower farming practices, including planting, cultivation, pest and disease management, and harvesting techniques.

Skills Needed: Proficiency in agronomy, horticulture, and floriculture principles. Continuous learning and staying updated on advancements in farming technology and techniques.

5. Labor and Human Resources

Assessment: Determine the availability of labor for farm operations, including planting, maintenance, harvesting, and packaging.

Skills Needed: Leadership and team management skills to effectively supervise and coordinate farm workers. Ability to recruit, train, and retain skilled labor.

6 Marketing and Sales Skills

Assessment: Assess your understanding of marketing strategies and sales channels for selling flowers, including direct sales, wholesale distribution, farmer's markets, and online platforms.

Skills Needed: Marketing research and analysis skills to identify target markets, consumer preferences, and competitive trends. Ability to develop branding, packaging, and promotional materials to attract customers.

7. Regulatory Compliance

Assessment: Determine your knowledge of regulatory requirements and permits for flower farming, including agricultural zoning, environmental regulations, pesticide use, and food safety standards.

Skills Needed: Understanding of legal and regulatory frameworks governing agriculture. Ability to navigate permit applications, inspections, and compliance procedures.

8. Risk Management

Assessment: Identify potential risks and challenges associated with flower farming, such as weather fluctuations, pest infestations, market volatility, and operational disruptions.

Skills Needed: Risk assessment and mitigation skills to develop contingency plans and strategies for minimizing losses. Flexibility and adaptability to respond to unforeseen challenges.

9. Networking and Collaborations

Assessment: Evaluate your ability to build relationships with industry stakeholders, including suppliers, buyers, fellow farmers, and agricultural organizations.

Skills Needed: Communication, negotiation, and networking skills to establish partnerships and collaborations that benefit your flower farm. Active participation in industry events, workshops, and community initiatives.

10. Time Management and Planning

Assessment: Assess your time management skills and ability to plan and prioritize tasks effectively to ensure the smooth operation of your flower farm.

Skills Needed: Organizational skills to develop production schedules, manage daily activities, and meet deadlines. Utilization of time-saving tools and techniques, such as crop planning software and task delegation.

Developing a Business Plan for Success in Flower Farm

A well-crafted business plan is essential for the success of any flower farming venture. It serves as a roadmap, guiding your decisions and actions to achieve your goals effectively. Below is a comprehensive guide on how to develop a business plan for your flower farming:

➢ **Executive Summary**

Provide a concise overview of your flower farming business, including its mission, vision, and objectives.

Summarize key elements of the business plan, such as target market, products and services, competitive advantages, and financial projections.

➤ Company Description

Describe your flower farming business in detail, including its legal structure, location, and history (if applicable).

Highlight the unique selling points of your flower farm, such as specialty flower varieties, sustainable farming practices, or direct-to-consumer sales approach.

➤ Market Analysis

Conduct a thorough analysis of the flower market, including trends, demand drivers, and competitive landscape.

Identify your target market segments, such as retail florists, event planners, wholesale distributors, or direct consumers.

Assess consumer preferences, pricing dynamics, and distribution channels relevant to your flower farming business.

➤ Products and Services

Outline the types of flowers you plan to cultivate, including both seasonal and specialty varieties.

Highlight any value-added services or products you offer, such as flower arrangements, bouquet subscriptions, or event floral design services.

Emphasize the quality, freshness, and uniqueness of your flowers compared to competitors.

➤ Marketing and Sales strategy

Define your marketing objectives and strategies for promoting your flower farm and products.

Identify marketing channels and tactics, such as social media, website, email newsletters, farmer's markets, or collaborations with local florists.

Develop a pricing strategy that reflects the value of your flowers while remaining competitive in the market.

➤ Operation Plan

Detail the day-to-day operations of your flower farm, including planting, cultivation, irrigation, pest and disease management, and harvesting.

Describe your production schedule and techniques for maximizing yield, quality, and efficiency.

Address logistical considerations, such as transportation, storage, and packaging of flowers for distribution.

➤ Management and Organizations

Introduce the key individuals involved in your flower farming business, including owners, managers, and key employees.

Outline their roles, responsibilities, and qualifications, emphasizing relevant experience and expertise in agriculture, horticulture, or business management.

Discuss your organizational structure, decision-making processes, and plans for hiring additional staff as needed.

➤ Financial plan

Prepare a comprehensive financial forecast, including startup costs, operating expenses, revenue projections, and cash flow analysis.

Estimate the cost of land acquisition or lease, equipment purchases or rentals, seeds, labor, utilities, marketing, and administrative expenses.

Calculate your break-even point and projected return on investment (ROI) to assess the financial viability of your flower farming business.

➤ Risk Management

Identify potential risks and challenges that may impact your flower farming business, such as adverse weather conditions, pest infestations, market volatility, or supply chain disruptions.

Develop risk mitigation strategies and contingency plans to minimize the impact of these risks on your operations and finances.

Consider purchasing insurance coverage, implementing diversification strategies, or establishing partnerships to mitigate specific risks.

➢ **Appendices**

Include supporting documents and additional information relevant to your flower farming business, such as resumes of key personnel, market research data, regulatory permits, or lease agreements.

Provide detailed financial statements, including balance sheets, income statements, and cash flow statements, to support your financial projections.

Regularly review and update your business plan as your flower farm grows and evolves, adjusting strategies and objectives to reflect changing market conditions and business goals. With a solid business plan in place, you'll be well-positioned to achieve sustainable growth and profitability in the competitive flower farming industry.

Legal and Regulatory Considerations in Flower Farming

Flower farming, like any agricultural activity, is subject to various legal and regulatory considerations that must be carefully navigated to ensure compliance and mitigate potential risks. These considerations encompass a range of issues, from land use and environmental regulations to labor laws and product safety standards.

One of the primary legal considerations in flower farming is **land use regulations.** Depending on the location of the farm, there may be zoning laws dictating where agricultural activities, including flower cultivation, are permitted. It's essential to verify that the chosen land is zoned appropriately for farming and obtain any necessary permits or approvals from local authorities.

Environmental regulations also play a significant role in flower farming, particularly concerning water usage, pesticide application, and soil conservation. Farmers must adhere to laws governing the use of water resources, such as obtaining permits for irrigation and complying with restrictions on water usage during drought conditions. Additionally, the application of pesticides and fertilizers is regulated to protect human health and the environment, requiring adherence to application rates, safety protocols, and record-keeping requirements.

Labor laws and regulations are another critical aspect of flower farming, especially for farms that rely on hired labor for planting, harvesting, and other tasks. Farmers must comply with employment laws regarding wages, working hours, safety standards, and worker protections. This includes ensuring fair wages, providing safe working conditions, and adhering to child labor laws and anti-discrimination policies.

Product safety and labeling regulations are essential considerations for flower farmers, particularly those selling directly to consumers or to businesses that serve the public. While flowers themselves are generally not subject to the same stringent regulations as food products, certain requirements may apply, such as labeling regulations for imported flowers or restrictions on the use of certain chemicals or treatments.

In addition to these specific legal considerations, flower farmers must also be aware of general business regulations and requirements, such as tax obligations, business licensing, and insurance coverage. Compliance with these regulations helps protect the business from legal liabilities and ensures smooth operations.

Overall, navigating the legal and regulatory landscape in flower farming requires diligence, attention to detail, and ongoing monitoring of changes in laws and regulations that may impact the business. By staying informed and proactive in addressing legal considerations, flower farmers can operate their businesses responsibly and sustainably while minimizing legal risks and maximizing compliance.

CHAPTER 2

Cultivating Profitable Flower Varieties

Flower farming presents a promising opportunity for agricultural entrepreneurs seeking to cultivate beauty while turning a profit. In recent years, the global demand for flowers has surged, driven by various factors such as increased consumer spending on aesthetics, growing awareness of the therapeutic benefits of flowers, and the rising popularity of floral arrangements in events and celebrations. In this chapter, we talk about cultivating profitable flowers in flower farming, exploring key considerations, strategies, and potential challenges in this dynamic industry.

Understanding the Market Dynamics

Before going into flower cultivation, it's crucial to grasp the intricacies of the flower market. The demand for flowers fluctuates seasonally and is influenced by factors such as cultural traditions, holidays, and special occasions. Different varieties of flowers command varying prices depending on factors such as rarity, fragrance, longevity, and aesthetic appeal. Market research is essential to identify profitable flower varieties, understand consumer preferences, and identify niche market opportunities.

Selecting Profitable Flower Varieties

Not all flowers are created equal when it comes to profitability. Some varieties are more sought after and command higher prices in the market. Factors to consider when selecting profitable flower varieties include market demand, growing conditions, production costs, and post-harvest longevity. Popular and high-value flowers such as roses, lilies, orchids, and peonies often offer lucrative opportunities for flower farmers.

Optimizing Cultivation Practices

Successful flower farming hinges on implementing effective cultivation practices that optimize yield, quality, and efficiency. This involves meticulous planning of planting schedules, soil preparation, irrigation management, pest and disease control, and post-harvest handling. Techniques such as crop rotation, companion planting, and integrated pest management can help minimize production costs and maximize profitability while maintaining sustainable farming practices.

Investing in Infrastructure and Technology

Investing in the right infrastructure and technology is essential for streamlining operations and enhancing productivity in flower farming. Greenhouses, irrigation systems, climate control equipment, and post-harvest facilities are critical investments that can improve crop yield, quality, and marketability. Additionally, leveraging technology such as precision farming tools, automated irrigation systems, and crop monitoring software can optimize resource utilization and decision-making, leading to higher profitability.

Marketing and Distribution Strategies

Effective marketing and distribution strategies are essential for maximizing the profitability of flower farming. Building strong relationships with wholesale buyers, florists, event planners, and retail outlets is crucial for securing consistent sales and achieving premium prices for your flowers. Direct-to-consumer sales channels such as farmer's markets, online platforms, and subscription services offer opportunities to capture higher margins and cultivate brand loyalty among customers.

Mitigating Risks and Challenges

While flower farming can be highly profitable, it's not without its risks and challenges. Factors such as adverse weather conditions, pest infestations, market volatility, and labor shortages can impact production and profitability. Implementing risk management strategies such as diversification, insurance coverage, and contingency planning can help mitigate these risks and safeguard the financial sustainability of the flower farming   enterprise.

Selecting High-Demand Flower Species

Selecting high-demand flower species is important for maximizing profitability and success in flower farming. High-demand flowers are those that are consistently sought after by consumers for various occasions, such as weddings, celebrations, and everyday floral arrangements. When choosing flower species to cultivate, it's essential to consider factors such as market demand, consumer preferences, growing conditions, and profitability. Here are some popular high-demand flower species that are widely sought after in the market:

1. Roses: Roses are timeless symbols of love, beauty, and romance, making them one of the most popular and high-demand flowers worldwide. With their wide range of colors, fragrances, and varieties, roses are a staple in floral arrangements for weddings, anniversaries, and special occasions.

2. Lilies: Lilies are prized for their elegant appearance, vibrant colors, and sweet fragrance, making them a favorite choice for bouquets, centerpieces, and floral displays. Asiatic lilies, Oriental lilies, and hybrid varieties are among the most popular types of lilies cultivated for commercial purposes.

3. Orchids: Orchids are exotic and captivating flowers known for their unique shapes, intricate patterns, and long-lasting blooms. With their wide range of colors and varieties, orchids are highly sought after for use in upscale floral arrangements, events, and decorative purposes.

4. Peonies: Peonies are beloved for their large, lush blooms, delicate fragrance, and romantic appeal. These luxurious flowers are in high demand for weddings, bridal bouquets, and floral gifts, especially during the peak peony season in late spring to early summer.

5. Tulips: Tulips are iconic spring flowers cherished for their vibrant colors, graceful petals, and symbolic meanings. These versatile flowers are popular for both indoor and outdoor decorations, such as flower beds, borders, and cut flower arrangements.

6. Sunflowers: Sunflowers exude warmth, happiness, and vitality, making them popular choices for adding a cheerful touch to floral arrangements and home decor. These vibrant flowers are especially sought after during the summer months for their bright and cheerful appearance

7. Gerbera Daisies: Gerbera daisies are known for their large, colorful blooms and long vase life, making them popular choices for bouquets, centerpieces, and floral arrangements. With their wide range of colors and playful appearance, gerbera daisies are versatile flowers that appeal to a broad range of consumers.

8. Hydrangeas: Hydrangeas are prized for their lush, voluminous blooms and vibrant colors, making them popular choices for wedding flowers, garden arrangements, and floral designs. These versatile flowers are available in various hues and are known for their longevity as cut flowers.

9. Carnations: Carnations are classic flowers cherished for their ruffled petals, sweet fragrance, and long-lasting blooms. These budget-friendly flowers are popular for use in bouquets, corsages, and floral arrangements for various occasions.

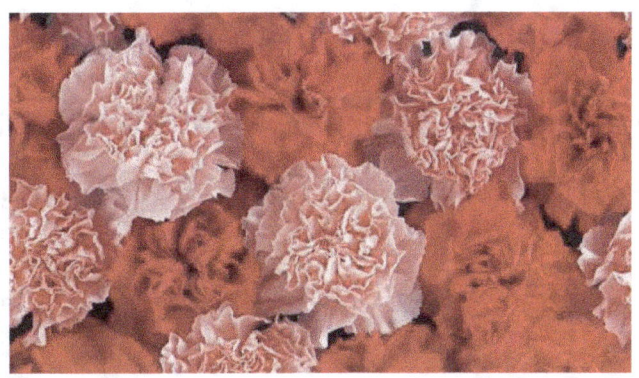

10. Calla Lilies: Calla lilies are elegant and sophisticated flowers prized for their graceful curves, trumpet-shaped blooms, and minimalist appeal. These versatile flowers are popular choices for bridal bouquets, wedding decor, and modern floral arrangements.

When selecting high-demand flower species for cultivation, it's essential to research market trends, consumer preferences, and regional demand to identify profitable opportunities. Additionally, consider factors such as growing conditions, production costs, and post-harvest handling requirements to ensure successful cultivation and maximize profitability in flower farming.

Understanding Seasonality and Market Trends

Understanding seasonality and market trends is essential for successful flower farming, as it allows farmers to align their cultivation practices with consumer demand and maximize profitability.

Seasonality

Seasonality refers to the natural fluctuations in flower availability and demand throughout the year, influenced by factors such as climate, holidays, and special occasions.

a. Seasonal Flower Availability: Different flower species have specific blooming seasons dictated by factors such as daylight length, temperature, and weather conditions. Understanding the seasonal availability of flowers is crucial for planning cultivation schedules and meeting consumer demand.

b. Peak Seasons: Certain flowers experience peak demand during specific seasons or holidays. For example, roses are in high demand during Valentine's Day and Mother's Day, while poinsettias are popular during the winter holiday season. By focusing on cultivating flowers that peak in demand during specific seasons, farmers can capitalize on market opportunities and maximize profits.

c. Off-Season Opportunities: While some flowers are associated with specific seasons, there are also opportunities to cultivate off-season or specialty flowers that command premium prices due to their rarity or uniqueness. For example, greenhouse cultivation allows farmers to produce flowers year-round, extending the availability of certain varieties beyond their natural blooming seasons.

d. Regional Variations: Seasonal patterns and consumer preferences may vary by region due to differences in climate, culture, and local traditions. Farmers should consider regional variations in seasonality and market demand when planning cultivation strategies and targeting specific markets.

Market Trends

Market trends, on the other hand, reflect broader shifts in consumer preferences, purchasing behavior, and industry dynamics.

a. Consumer Preferences: Consumer preferences for flower types, colors, and arrangements are constantly evolving, driven by factors such as lifestyle trends, fashion influences, and cultural shifts. Farmers should stay attuned to changing consumer preferences and adjust their product offerings accordingly to meet demand.

b. Sustainable and Locally Grown Flowers: There is a growing demand for sustainably grown and locally sourced flowers, driven by increasing environmental awareness and concerns about carbon footprint and pesticide use in flower production. Farmers who adopt sustainable farming practices and promote their products as locally grown can capitalize on this trend and differentiate themselves in the market.

c. Specialty and Niche Markets: There is a rising demand for specialty and niche flowers, including heirloom varieties, rare species, and unique cultivars. These flowers often appeal to niche markets such as luxury weddings, upscale events, and specialty florists, offering opportunities for higher margins and premium pricing.

d. Online and Direct-to-Consumer Sales: The rise of e-commerce and direct-to-consumer sales channels has transformed the flower market, providing farmers with opportunities to reach customers directly through online platforms, subscription services, and farmer's markets. Farmers who embrace digital marketing and e-commerce can expand their reach and tap into new market segments.

e. Customization and Personalization: Consumers increasingly seek personalized and customized floral arrangements tailored to their individual preferences and occasions. Farmers who offer customizable options, such as bouquet subscriptions, DIY flower kits, and bespoke floral designs, can cater to this demand and enhance customer satisfaction.

Various flower types and their seasonal availability along with their market trends (what they can be used for and when they can be used)

Spring Flowers

Tulips: Tulips are iconic spring flowers available in a wide range of colors and varieties. They are popular for floral arrangements, bouquets, and garden displays during the spring season.

Daffodils: Daffodils are cheerful spring flowers known for their bright yellow blooms and trumpet-shaped petals. They are commonly used in Easter arrangements and springtime floral displays.

Hyacinths: Hyacinths are fragrant spring flowers prized for their vibrant colors and sweet scent. They are popular for indoor and outdoor decorations, as well as for adding fragrance to floral arrangements.

Summer Flowers

Roses: Roses are classic summer flowers that bloom abundantly during the warm months. They are highly sought after for weddings, special occasions, and romantic gestures, with a wide variety of colors and fragrances available.

Sunflowers: Sunflowers are vibrant summer flowers known for their large, sunny blooms and cheerful appearance. They are popular for outdoor decorations, bouquets, and floral arrangements during the summer season.

Zinnias: Zinnias are colorful summer flowers available in a wide range of hues, shapes, and sizes. They are prized for their long-lasting blooms and are popular for garden borders, cut flower arrangements, and pollinator gardens.

Fall Flowers

Chrysanthemums: Chrysanthemums, or mums, are quintessential fall flowers known for their rich colors and prolific blooms. They are popular for autumnal decorations, seasonal displays, and floral arrangements for Thanksgiving and harvest festivals.

Dahlias: Dahlias are showy fall flowers prized for their intricate blooms and vibrant colors. They are popular for late-season floral arrangements, weddings, and special events, with a wide variety of shapes and sizes available.

Asters: Asters are delicate fall flowers known for their daisy-like blooms and pastel hues. They are popular for adding a touch of color to autumnal bouquets, garden borders, and floral designs.

Winter Flowers

Poinsettias: Poinsettias are iconic winter flowers associated with the holiday season. They are prized for their vibrant red bracts and are commonly used as decorations for Christmas celebrations and festive displays.

Hellebores: Hellebores, or Christmas roses, are winter-blooming flowers known for their elegant blooms and shade tolerance. They are popular for adding color to winter gardens, floral arrangements, and indoor decorations.

Cyclamen: Cyclamen are winter-blooming flowers prized for their vibrant colors and unique, swept-back petals. They are popular for indoor decorations, potted plants, and winter floral arrangements.

Year-Round and Specialty Flowers

Orchids: Orchids are exotic flowers available year-round and prized for their intricate blooms and long-lasting beauty. They are popular for weddings, upscale events, and floral arrangements that require a touch of elegance and sophistication.

Gerbera Daisies: Gerbera daisies are cheerful flowers available year-round in a wide range of colors and sizes. They are popular for bouquets, centerpieces, and floral designs that call for bold, vibrant blooms.

Ranunculus: Ranunculus are specialty flowers prized for their delicate, layered petals and wide color palette. They are popular for weddings, bridal bouquets, and floral arrangements that require a romantic and feminine touch.

These examples illustrate how different flowers have distinct seasonality and market trends, influencing their availability and demand throughout the year. By understanding these patterns and trends, flower farmers can strategically plan their cultivation and marketing strategies to meet consumer demand and maximize profitability.

Maximizing Yield and Quality Through Cultivation Techniques

Maximizing yield and quality through cultivation techniques is essential for flower farmers to achieve profitability and success in their operations. By implementing effective cultivation practices, farmers can optimize plant growth, minimize losses, and produce high-quality flowers that meet market demand.

Soil Preparation

Soil Testing: Conduct soil tests to assess nutrient levels, pH, and texture. Based on the results, amend the soil as needed to ensure optimal nutrient availability and soil structure for plant growth.

Organic Matter: Incorporate organic matter such as compost, manure, or cover crops into the soil to improve fertility, moisture retention, and microbial activity. Organic matter also helps suppress weeds and reduce the need for synthetic fertilizers.

Irrigation Management

Watering Schedule: Establish a regular watering schedule based on plant needs, soil moisture levels, and weather conditions. Avoid overwatering, which can lead to root rot and fungal diseases, or underwatering, which can stress plants and reduce yield.

Drip Irrigation: Install drip irrigation systems to deliver water directly to the plant roots, minimizing water waste and optimizing water efficiency. Drip irrigation also reduces the risk of foliar diseases and weed growth compared to overhead irrigation methods.

Fertilization Practices

Balanced Nutrition: Provide plants with a balanced supply of essential nutrients, including nitrogen, phosphorus, potassium, and micronutrients, to support healthy growth and flowering. Use slow-release organic fertilizers or liquid fertilizers applied at appropriate rates to avoid nutrient deficiencies or excesses.

Foliar Feeding: Apply liquid fertilizers or micronutrient sprays directly to the leaves through foliar feeding to enhance nutrient uptake and address nutrient deficiencies. Foliar feeding can supplement soil fertility and improve plant health and vigor.

Pest and Disease Management

Integrated Pest Management (IPM): Implement IPM strategies to control pests and diseases while minimizing environmental impact and preserving beneficial organisms. This includes cultural practices, biological controls, mechanical methods, and targeted pesticide applications as a last resort.

Crop Rotation: Rotate flower crops with other non-host plants to disrupt pest and disease cycles and reduce buildup of soil-borne pathogens. Crop rotation also helps maintain soil fertility and structure over time.

Pruning and Training

Deadheading: Remove spent flowers regularly through deadheading to encourage continuous blooming and prevent seed formation, which can divert energy away from flower production. Deadheading also improves plant appearance and prolongs flowering duration.

Training Techniques: Train plants to grow in desired shapes or structures through techniques such as staking, trellising, or pinching. Training techniques improve light penetration, air circulation, and flower quality, leading to higher yields and better overall plant health.

Harvesting and Post- Harvesting Handling

Optimal Timing: Harvest flowers at the optimal stage of maturity when blooms are fully developed but not overripe. Timing varies by flower species and variety, so monitor plants closely and harvest accordingly to maximize vase life and quality.

Proper Handling: Handle harvested flowers gently to avoid damage to petals, stems, or foliage. Use sharp, clean tools to make clean cuts and immediately place harvested flowers in clean water with floral preservatives to extend vase life and maintain freshness.

CHAPTER 3

Marketing and Sales Strategies for Flower Farmers

In the competitive world of flower farming, effective marketing and sales strategies are essential for success. Flower farmers not only need to produce high-quality blooms but also need to connect with customers, differentiate their products, and maximize sales opportunities. This chapter explores various marketing and sales strategies specifically for flower farmers, highlighting key considerations, tactics, and best practices to effectively promote and sell your flowers.

Understanding the Flower Market

Before diving into marketing and sales strategies, it's crucial for flower farmers to understand the dynamics of the flower market. This includes analyzing consumer preferences, identifying target market segments, and staying informed about industry trends and competitive landscape. By understanding the market, flower farmers can tailor their marketing efforts to meet customer needs and capitalize on opportunities.

Developing a Unique Value Proposition

One of the first steps in crafting a successful marketing strategy is defining a unique value proposition that sets your flower farm apart from competitors. This could include factors such as organic or sustainable farming practices, specialty flower varieties, exceptional quality, or personalized customer service. A clear and compelling value proposition helps differentiate your farm and attracts customers who resonate with your brand.

Utilizing Multiple Sales Channels

Flower farmers should explore multiple sales channels to reach a diverse customer base and maximize sales opportunities. This could include selling directly to consumers through farmer's markets, roadside stands, or on-farm retail sales. Additionally, farmers can establish partnerships with florists, event planners, restaurants, and other businesses to wholesale flowers. Online sales through e-commerce platforms or subscription services are also increasingly popular options for reaching customers.

Building an Online Presence

In today's digital age, having a strong online presence is essential for reaching customers and promoting your flower farm. This includes having a professional website showcasing your products, services, and farm story. Utilize social media platforms such as Instagram, Facebook, and Pinterest to share photos of your flowers, engage with customers, and build a loyal following. Regularly update your online channels with fresh content to keep customers informed and engaged.

Effective Branding and Packaging

Branding plays a crucial role in attracting customers and building brand recognition for your flower farm. Develop a cohesive brand identity that reflects your farm's values, personality, and unique selling points. This includes designing a memorable logo, selecting a distinctive color palette, and creating visually appealing packaging for your flowers. Consistent branding helps reinforce your farm's identity and leaves a lasting impression on customers.

Implementing Promotional Strategies

Promotional strategies such as discounts, promotions, and special offers can help drive sales and attract new customers. Consider offering seasonal promotions, bundle deals, or loyalty programs to incentivize repeat purchases and reward customer loyalty. Collaborate with local businesses or participate in community events to increase visibility and reach new customers through cross-promotion.

Collecting Customers Feedback and Reviews

Feedback from customers is invaluable for improving products and services and building customer loyalty. Encourage customers to provide feedback through surveys, reviews, or testimonials. Actively listen to customer feedback and use it to identify areas for improvement, address customer concerns, and refine your offerings. Positive reviews and testimonials can also serve as powerful endorsements and boost credibility and trust in your flower farm.

Measuring and Analyzing Results

It's essential to track and measure the effectiveness of your marketing and sales efforts to identify what's working well and what can be improved. Use analytics tools to monitor website traffic, social media engagement, and sales performance. Analyze key metrics such as conversion rates, customer acquisition costs, and return on investment (ROI) to evaluate the success of your marketing campaigns and make data-driven decisions.

Building Your Brand and Market Presence

Effective branding helps convey your farm's unique story, values, and offerings, while a robust market presence ensures visibility and recognition among target audiences. Here's a comprehensive guide on how you can build your brand and market presence:

Define your Brand Identity

- **Mission and Values:** Start by defining your farm's mission and values. What drives your passion for flower farming? What principles guide your farming practices? Communicate these values clearly to establish an emotional connection with customers who share your beliefs.

- **Farm Story:** Share the story behind your farm, including its history, founders, and journey. Highlight what sets your farm apart, such as sustainable farming practices, unique flower varieties, or a commitment to community engagement.

- **Visual Identity:** Develop a cohesive visual identity that reflects your brand's personality and values. This includes designing a memorable logo, selecting a distinctive color palette, and creating consistent branding elements for packaging, signage, and marketing materials.

Know Your Audience

- **Customer Segmentation:** Identify your target audience and segment them based on demographics, psychographics, and buying behaviors. Understand their preferences, needs, and pain points to tailor your marketing messages and offerings accordingly.

- **Market Research:** Conduct market research to gain insights into industry trends, competitor offerings, and customer preferences. Stay informed about changing consumer behaviors, emerging market opportunities, and evolving industry dynamics.

Establish an Online Presence

- **Professional Website:** Create a professional website that showcases your farm's story, products, and services. Ensure that your website is user-friendly, visually appealing, and optimized for search engines to attract organic traffic.

- **Social Media Engagement:** Leverage social media platforms such as Instagram, Facebook, and Pinterest to share captivating photos of your flowers, behind-the-scenes glimpses of farm life, and engaging content that resonates with your audience. Build a community of followers and foster meaningful interactions to enhance brand visibility and engagement.

Showcase Your Products

- **High-Quality Imagery:** Invest in professional photography to showcase your flowers in their best light. High-quality, visually stunning images attract attention and evoke emotions, enticing customers to explore your products further.

- **Product Packaging:** Design attractive and eco-friendly packaging for your flowers that aligns with your brand identity. Consider using branded labels, wraps, or containers that enhance the presentation and perceived value of your products.

Build Good Relationships with Your Customers

- **Customer Engagement:** Cultivate relationships with your customers through personalized communication, exceptional service, and attentive support. Respond promptly to inquiries, address customer feedback, and go the extra mile to exceed expectations.

- **Community Involvement:** Get involved in your local community by participating in farmer's markets, festivals, and events. Build relationships with other local businesses, florists, and event planners to expand your network and reach new customers through collaborations and partnerships.

Collect and Showcase Testimonials

- **Customer Testimonials:** Collect testimonials and reviews from satisfied customers to showcase the positive experiences and outcomes associated with your products and services. Display these testimonials on your website, social media profiles, and marketing materials to build credibility and trust with potential customers.

Monitor and Adapt

- **Analytics and Feedback:** Use analytics tools to track key performance metrics such as website traffic, social media engagement, and sales conversions. Monitor customer feedback, market trends, and competitor activities to identify areas for improvement and opportunities for growth.

- **Adaptation:** Continuously refine and adapt your branding and marketing strategies based on data-driven insights and evolving market dynamics. Stay agile and responsive to changes in consumer preferences, industry trends, and competitive landscape to maintain relevance and competitive advantage.

Developing Effective Sales Channels

To generate reasonable sales on flower farming, you need to try various channels and means to reach your prospective customers. By developing effective sales channels and leveraging diverse distribution channels, flower farmers can reach a wider audience, increase sales volume, and build a sustainable and profitable business. It's essential to continuously evaluate and optimize sales channels based on customer feedback, market trends, and business objectives to maximize revenue and long-term success. A few channels to utilize have been prepared for you.

Direct-to-Consumer Sales

Set up an on-farm retail stand or flower shop where customers can purchase fresh flowers directly from the farm. Create an inviting and aesthetically pleasing retail space that showcases your flowers and farm story.

Participate in local farmers markets to sell your flowers directly to consumers. Farmers markets provide an excellent opportunity to connect with customers, build relationships, and gain exposure within the community.

Offer U-pick or pick-your-own flower experiences where customers can visit the farm and harvest their own flowers. This interactive and hands-on experience adds value and creates memorable moments for customers.

Wholesale and Retail Partnerships

Partner with local florists to supply them with fresh flowers for their floral arrangements, bouquets, and designs. Build relationships with florists who appreciate locally grown, high-quality flowers and offer them competitive pricing and reliable service.

Collaborate with event planners, wedding coordinators, and party organizers to supply flowers for weddings, special events, and corporate functions. Position your farm as a preferred supplier for events seeking locally sourced and seasonal blooms.

Approach retail outlets such as grocery stores, garden centers, and boutique shops to stock your flowers on their shelves. Provide retailers with attractive displays, signage, and promotional materials to drive sales and attract customers.

Online Sales Channels

Develop an e-commerce website where customers can browse your flower offerings, place orders, and arrange for delivery or pickup. Invest in user-friendly design, secure payment processing, and seamless navigation to enhance the online shopping experience.

List your flowers on online marketplaces such as Etsy, Amazon Handmade, or local online platforms specializing in artisanal products. Leverage the reach and visibility of these platforms to reach a broader audience and attract online customers.

Offer flower subscription services where customers can sign up to receive regular deliveries of fresh flowers on a weekly, bi-weekly, or monthly basis. Subscription services provide a predictable revenue stream and cultivate loyal, repeat customers.

Corporate and Institutional Sales

Supply flowers to restaurants, hotels, and hospitality establishments to enhance their ambiance and décor. Create customized floral arrangements tailored to the aesthetic and branding of each establishment.

Target corporate clients for bulk flower orders for office décor, corporate events, client gifts, and employee appreciation. Develop relationships with corporate buyers and offer personalized service and competitive pricing to win their business.

Community Engagement and Special Events

Participate in community events, festivals, fairs, and fundraisers to showcase your flowers and engage with potential customers. Set up a booth or display to promote your farm and sell flowers directly to event attendees.

Host workshops, classes, and farm tours to educate the community about flower farming, floral design, and gardening. Offer hands-on experiences where participants can learn to arrange flowers or create their own bouquets.

Customer Relationship Management

Provide personalized service and attentive support to customers to build rapport and foster loyalty. Respond promptly to inquiries, accommodate special requests, and exceed customer expectations to create positive experiences.

Implement customer loyalty programs to reward repeat purchases and encourage customer retention. Offer discounts, special offers, or exclusive perks to loyal customers as a token of appreciation for their continued support.

Utilizing Online Platforms and Social Media for Promotion

Utilizing online platforms and social media for promotion is essential for flower farmers to expand their reach, connect with customers, and showcase their products and services effectively in the digital age. With the widespread use of the internet and social media platforms, farmers can leverage these channels to engage with their target audience, drive traffic to their website or farm, and ultimately increase sales. To do this you have to:

Establish a Strong Online Presence

Create a professional website that serves as a central hub for your flower farm online. Your website should showcase your farm's story, highlight your products and services, and provide essential information such as contact details, operating hours, and location.

Ensure that your website is user-friendly, visually appealing, and optimized for both desktop and mobile devices. Use clear navigation, high-quality images, and concise copy to create a seamless and engaging browsing experience for visitors.

Leverage Social Media Platforms

Instagram: Instagram is a visual-centric platform ideal for showcasing beautiful flower arrangements, behind-the-scenes glimpses of farm life, and customer testimonials. Use hashtags strategically to increase visibility and engage with your audience through comments, likes, and direct messages.

Facebook: Facebook is a versatile platform where you can share a mix of content, including photos, videos, blog posts, and event announcements. Create a Facebook page for your flower farm and post regularly to keep your audience informed and engaged.

Pinterest: Pinterest is a popular platform for discovering and saving visual inspiration, making it an excellent tool for promoting your flower farm. Create boards featuring your flowers, wedding inspiration, garden tips, and DIY floral arrangements to attract Pinterest users interested in these topics.

YouTube: Consider creating video content for YouTube showcasing farm tours, flower arranging tutorials, and behind-the-scenes footage of your farming operations. Video content can help humanize your brand and establish a deeper connection with your audience.

Engage With Your Audience

Monitor your social media accounts regularly and respond promptly to comments, messages, and inquiries from your audience. Engage in conversations, answer questions, and show appreciation for comments to foster a sense of community and build relationships with your followers.

Encourage your customers to share photos of your flowers on social media and tag your farm. Repost user-generated content on your own accounts to showcase customer experiences and foster a sense of community among your followers.

Share Valuable Contents

Share educational content related to flower farming, gardening tips, floral design techniques, and flower care instructions. Position yourself as a trusted authority in your niche by providing valuable information that resonates with your audience.

Offer glimpses into the daily operations of your farm through behind-the-scenes content such as farm tours, meet-the-farmer interviews, and day-inthe-life stories. Humanize your brand and build authenticity by sharing the people and stories behind your flowers.

Run Promotions and Contests

Promotional Campaigns: Run promotional campaigns or sales events exclusively for your social media followers to incentivize engagement and drive traffic to your farm. Offer discounts, giveaways, or special offers to encourage followers to take action and make a purchase.

Contests and Giveaways: Host contests or giveaways on social media where participants can enter to win prizes such as free flower bouquets, farm tours, or flower arranging workshops. Contests are an effective way to generate excitement, increase brand awareness, and attract new followers.

Measure and Analyze Results

Use analytics tools provided by social media platforms and website analytics software to track key metrics such as engagement, reach, website traffic, and conversion rates. Analyze the performance of your social media campaigns and website content to identify trends, insights, and areas for improvement.

Based on your analysis, iterate and refine your social media and online marketing strategies to optimize performance and achieve your business goals. Experiment with different types of content, posting schedules, and promotional tactics to see what resonates best with your audience.

CHAPTER 4

Financial Management and Growth Strategies

Effective financial management and growth strategies are vital for the success and sustainability of flower farming businesses. Flower farmers must carefully manage their finances, make informed decisions, and implement growth-oriented strategies to thrive in a competitive market. This comprehensive chapter explores various financial management practices and growth strategies tailored specifically for flower farming businesses, providing actionable insights and best practices to achieve financial stability and drive business growth.

Financial Management Practices

- **Budgeting and Forecasting:** Develop detailed budgets and financial forecasts to plan and allocate resources effectively. Consider factors such as production costs, labor expenses, equipment maintenance, and marketing expenses when creating budgets. Regularly review and update budgets to reflect changes in market conditions and business needs.

- **Cash Flow Management:** Monitor cash flow closely to ensure sufficient liquidity for day-to-day operations and seasonal fluctuations. Implement strategies to optimize cash flow, such as managing accounts receivable and payable efficiently, negotiating favorable payment terms with suppliers, and maintaining a cash reserve for emergencies.

- **Cost Control:** Identify cost-saving opportunities and implement measures to control expenses without compromising quality. Evaluate spending on inputs such as seeds, fertilizers, and pesticides, and explore ways to minimize waste, improve efficiency, and negotiate better pricing with suppliers.

- **Profitability Analysis:** Conduct regular profitability analysis to evaluate the financial performance of different flower varieties, products, and sales channels. Identify high-margin products and focus on scaling those offerings to maximize profitability. Use profitability insights to make data-driven decisions about pricing, production planning, and resource allocation.

- **Investment Planning:** Evaluate investment opportunities to support business growth and expansion. Consider investments in infrastructure upgrades, technology adoption, equipment purchases, and greenhouse expansion to increase productivity, enhance product quality, and streamline operations. Conduct thorough cost-benefit analysis and assess the potential return on investment (ROI) before making investment decisions.

Growth Strategies

- **Market Expansion:** Explore opportunities to expand into new geographic markets or target new customer segments. Identify underserved market niches or emerging trends in the floral industry and tailor your products and marketing strategies to capitalize on these opportunities.

- **Product Diversification:** Diversify your product offerings to appeal to a broader range of customers and mitigate risks associated with fluctuations in demand or market conditions. Experiment with new flower varieties, specialty products, or value-added services such as flower arranging workshops, subscription services, or event planning.

- **Brand Building and Marketing:** Invest in brand-building initiatives and marketing efforts to enhance brand visibility, attract customers, and differentiate your flower farm from competitors. Develop a compelling brand story, create engaging content, and leverage digital marketing channels such as social media, email marketing, and search engine optimization (SEO) to reach and engage with your target audience effectively.

- **Strategic Partnerships:** Forge strategic partnerships with complementary businesses such as florists, event planners, garden centers, and wedding venues to expand your reach and access new customer markets. Collaborate on joint marketing campaigns, cross-promotional activities, or co-branded product offerings to leverage each other's strengths and resources.

- **Customer Relationship Management:** Prioritize customer satisfaction and loyalty by providing exceptional service, personalized experiences, and ongoing communication. Build strong relationships with customers through loyalty programs, exclusive offers, and regular updates on new products or promotions. Encourage customer feedback and use it to continuously improve your products and services.

Budgeting and Cost Analysis for Flower Farming

Budgeting and cost analysis are fundamental components of financial management for flower farming businesses. Proper budgeting allows flower farmers to plan and allocate resources effectively, while cost analysis helps identify areas for optimization and cost-saving opportunities.

1. Establishing a Budget

Begin by estimating your expected revenue based on historical sales data, market trends, and anticipated demand for your flowers. Consider factors such as seasonality, holidays, and special events that may impact sales.

Identify and categorize all operational expenses associated with flower farming, including but not limited to:

- Seed and bulb purchases
- Soil amendments and fertilizers
- Irrigation systems and water costs
- Equipment maintenance and repairs
- Labor costs (wages, benefits, payroll taxes)
- Utilities (electricity, heating, cooling)
- Packaging materials
- Marketing and advertising expenses
- Insurance and permits
- Rent or mortgage payments for land or greenhouse space

Capital Expenditures: Consider any one-time or periodic investments in capital assets such as greenhouse construction or equipment purchases. Allocate funds for these expenditures based on their estimated cost and anticipated timing.

Contingency Reserve: Set aside a portion of your budget for unexpected expenses or emergencies to ensure financial stability and resilience in case of unforeseen challenges.

2. Monitoring and Tracking Expenses

Record-Keeping: Maintain detailed records of all expenses incurred throughout the growing season, including receipts, invoices, and transaction logs. Use accounting software or spreadsheets to organize and track expenses by category for easy analysis.

Regular Reviews: Review your budget and actual expenses regularly to monitor variances and identify any deviations from the planned budget. Compare actual spending to budgeted amounts and investigate any significant discrepancies.

Adjustments as Needed: Be prepared to adjust your budget as needed based on changing circumstances, such as unexpected expenses, revenue fluctuations, or shifts in market conditions. Prioritize spending on essential items while identifying opportunities to trim costs or reallocate resources where possible.

3. Cost Analysis and Optimization

Analyze your cost structure to identify the primary cost drivers impacting your flower farming operations. Common cost drivers in flower farming may include seed and bulb costs, labor expenses, irrigation and water usage, and energy costs for heating or cooling greenhouse facilities.

Conduct a cost-volume-profit (CVP) analysis to assess the relationship between costs, sales volume, and profitability. Determine your breakeven point—the level of sales needed to cover fixed and variable costs—and identify opportunities to improve profitability through increased sales or cost reduction measures.

Compare your costs to industry benchmarks or competitors' practices to identify areas where your farm may be over-spending or under-performing. Look for opportunities to adopt best practices, streamline processes, and implement cost-saving initiatives to improve efficiency and competitiveness.

Explore ways to improve efficiency and productivity in your farming operations to reduce costs and maximize profitability. This could include optimizing planting schedules, reducing water and energy usage, minimizing waste, and implementing technology solutions to automate tasks and streamline workflows.

4. Long-Term Planning and Investment

Capital Budgeting: Evaluate potential investments in capital assets such as greenhouse expansions, equipment upgrades, or technology investments. Conduct a cost-benefit analysis to assess the potential return on investment (ROI) and prioritize projects based on their impact on productivity, profitability, and long-term growth.

Sustainable Practices: Consider the long-term environmental and financial benefits of adopting sustainable farming practices such as organic cultivation methods, water conservation measures, and renewable energy sources. While initial costs may be higher, sustainable practices can yield cost savings, reduce environmental impact, and enhance the overall value proposition of your farm.

Risk Management: Factor in risk management considerations when budgeting and planning for the future. Identify potential risks such as adverse weather conditions, crop diseases, market volatility, or regulatory changes, and develop contingency plans to mitigate these risks and safeguard your farm's financial stability.

Pricing Strategies for Profitability

Flower farming represents a delicate balance between artistry and economics. While the beauty and fragrance of flowers captivate consumers, the profitability of flower farming hinges significantly on pricing strategies.

Understanding the importance of strategic pricing and implementing appropriate techniques can not only ensure sustainable business growth but also enhance profitability in the competitive floral market.

Importance of Pricing Strategies

Pricing directly influences revenue generation. Well-designed pricing strategies can help flower farmers optimize sales volumes and capture maximum value from their products.

Competitive Advantage: In a crowded market, pricing serves as a key differentiator. Strategic pricing allows farmers to stand out from competitors and attract customers based on perceived value rather than just price.

Profitability Enhancement: Effective pricing strategies directly impact the bottom line. By aligning prices with production costs, market demand, and consumer preferences, flower farmers can improve profitability and ensure long-term sustainability.

Market Positioning: Pricing strategies communicate brand positioning and quality perception. Whether positioned as premium, mid-range, or budget-friendly, pricing influences how consumers perceive a flower farm's products and services.

Pricing Strategies for Profitability

Cost-Based Pricing:

- Calculate production costs, including seedlings, labor, fertilizers, and overhead expenses.
- Add a desired profit margin to determine the minimum selling price.
- Adjust pricing periodically to reflect changes in input costs or market conditions.

Market-Based Pricing:

- Analyze market demand and competitor pricing to set prices competitively.
- Consider seasonal fluctuations and trends in the floral market.
- Leverage consumer research and feedback to understand price sensitivity and willingness to pay.

Value-Based Pricing:

- Focus on the perceived value of flowers rather than production costs alone.
- Highlight unique qualities, such as freshness, fragrance, and variety assortment, to justify premium pricing.
- Offer bundled packages or customization options to enhance perceived value and justify higher prices.

Dynamic Pricing:

- Implement dynamic pricing strategies based on real-time market data and demand fluctuations.
- Utilize pricing algorithms and software to adjust prices dynamically in response to changing market conditions.
- Offer discounts or promotions during off-peak seasons or to clear excess inventory.

Psychological Pricing:

- Utilize pricing tactics that appeal to consumers' psychological biases and perceptions.
- Set prices just below round numbers (e.g., $9.99 instead of $10) to create the perception of a better deal.
- Offer tiered pricing options (e.g., small, medium, large bouquets) to provide choice and cater to different budget preferences.

Scaling Up Your Flower Farm Business for Long-Term Success

Scaling up a flower farming business involves expanding operations to increase production capacity, reach new markets, and improve profitability. Here's a detailed guide on how to scale up your flower farming business effectively:

Evaluate Current Operations: Before scaling up, conduct a thorough assessment of your current operations. Identify strengths, weaknesses, and areas for improvement. Understand your production capacity, resource availability, and market demand.

Develop a Growth Strategy: Define clear objectives and goals for scaling up your business. Determine the desired scale of expansion, target markets, and timeline for implementation. Consider factors such as investment requirements, operational changes, and potential risks.

Invest in Infrastructure: Scaling up may require investments in infrastructure, such as expanding greenhouse facilities, acquiring additional land, or upgrading equipment. Evaluate the cost-benefit of these investments and prioritize based on their impact on production efficiency and quality.

Optimize Production Processes: Streamline production processes to increase efficiency and productivity. Implement best practices for planting, irrigation, fertilization, pest control, and harvesting. Invest in technology and automation to reduce labor costs and minimize waste.

Diversify Product Offerings: Explore opportunities to diversify your product offerings to meet diverse customer needs and preferences. Introduce new flower varieties, bouquet arrangements, or value-added products such as dried flowers, potpourri, or floral arrangements for special occasions.

Expand Market Reach: Identify new market opportunities to expand your customer base. Explore avenues such as online sales platforms, farmer's markets, floral shops, event planners, and wholesale distributors. Develop marketing strategies to promote your products and build brand awareness in target markets.

Build Strategic Partnerships: Collaborate with other businesses, suppliers, and industry partners to leverage resources, expand distribution channels, and access new markets. Forge strategic partnerships with florists, wedding planners, event organizers, and retail outlets to increase sales and visibility.

Focus on Quality and Customer Service: Maintain a strong focus on product quality and customer service as you scale up your operations. Ensure that your flowers meet high standards of freshness, fragrance, and appearance to retain customer loyalty and satisfaction.

Monitor Performance Metrics: Establish key performance indicators (KPIs) to track the progress of your scaling efforts. Monitor metrics such as production output, sales revenue, customer acquisition, and profitability. Use data analytics to identify trends, opportunities, and areas for improvement.

Adapt and Iterate: Scaling up is an iterative process that requires flexibility and adaptability. Be prepared to adjust your strategies based on market feedback, changing conditions, and lessons learned from experience.

Continuously evaluate the effectiveness of your scaling efforts and make necessary adjustments to optimize results.

CONCLUSION

As you close the final pages of this book on flower farming for profit, it's time to reflect on the journey we've embarked upon together—a journey filled with vibrant colors, delicate fragrances, and the promise of prosperity.

Throughout our exploration of the world of flower farming, we've delved deep into the soil, uncovering the secrets of cultivation, nurturing, and harvesting that transform humble seeds into blossoming beauties. We've witnessed the magic of nature at work, marveling at the intricate processes that bring each petal to life and fill the world with joy and wonder.

But our journey has been more than just a botanical adventure—it has been a quest for success, a pursuit of profitability in the flourishing floral industry. We've learned that flower farming is not just an art—it's a business, one that requires dedication, innovation, and a keen eye for opportunity.

As we reach the conclusion of this book, I want to leave you with a sense of empowerment, knowing that you have the knowledge, skills, and inspiration to cultivate your own path to prosperity in the world of flower farming. Whether you're a seasoned grower looking to expand your operations or a budding entrepreneur eager to sow the seeds of success, remember that the possibilities are endless, and the rewards are bountiful.

So, as you venture forth into the fields of flower farming, remember to dream big, think creatively, and never underestimate the power of a single seed to transform your world. With passion as your compass and perseverance as your guide, there's no limit to what you can achieve in this blooming industry.

And so, dear reader, as you turn the final page of this book, I invite you to take a moment to breathe in the fragrance of possibility, to embrace the beauty of potential, and to envision the future of your flower farming journey—a future filled with abundance, prosperity, and the sweet scent of success.

Thank you for joining me on this incredible odyssey through the world of flower farming. May your fields be forever in bloom, and may your harvests be plentiful. Here's to your success, your prosperity, and your ever-growing love affair with the art and science of flower farming. Happy farming!

www.ingramcontent.com/pod-product-compliance
Lightning Source LLC
Chambersburg PA
CBHW081141290526
45795CB00006B/2324